REMEMBER ME

TJ

ISBN 979-888521593-0

Contents

Contents

REMEMBER ME.

- Poems by TJ

Acknowledgements

No matter how the curtain of rain descends and makes way for a kaleidoscopic rainbow, one cant forget that it all begins with a single drop of rain.

Likewise, an encouraging word, a pat on the back, and the first step is all that it takes to nestle in the arms of success and shape your dreams.

I apologize, thank and dedicate this book to my son, Jadon for cheering me throughout my journey, believing that this would be a kids comic strip.

Author Bio

TJ lives in Pune with her exceptionally noisy and loving family. Before she started her writing journey, she worked in the IT industry for 10 years. After that, just to make things difficult for herself, she got her graduate and post graduate degree in English Literature.

Much to her family's embarrassment she no longer remembers what 'IT' in IT industry stands for. Only her son doesn't seem to mind and is her most loyal companion to binge watch cartoon shows and read comic books. When she isn't writing, reading or binge watching shows, she spends majority of her time daydreaming about chocolate cakes.

Her poems speak of wishes, hopes, dreams and lots of dandelions but in real life she's never seen a shooting star nor a dandelion.

If you wish to help TJ differentiate between grass and dandelion, you can reach her through email at 13TJade@gmail.com

DARKNESS

1. TINY LITTLE HANDS

Cloaked in dirt, tiny little hands.
We endlessly beg and seek refuge.
Soaked in fear, which nobody understands.
We tirelessly work, unable to refuse.

Burdened with living, denied to die.
We salvage waste and knight the scavenger.
Riddled with hunger, hesitant to cry.
We rummage through scraps and nourish the slum-dweller.

Trained to steal, but its all for a meal.
Feigned indifference, too scared to feel.
A corrupt touch, compliant to labour of lust.
An unkempt truth, derelict cradle of rust.

Destiny lines masked under a life of toil.
We crave for warmth, not the burn of parched soil.
Orphaned twins, detained for crimes unknown.
Hold us a while, for we are forsaken and alone.

2. BURDEN

Burden isn't what you carry-on your back,
it's the pain that you stash deep in your heart.
Darkness isn't when life turns pitch black,
it's when your shadow engulfs your heart.

Despair isn't when your hope is dwindling away,
it's when your tears are buried beneath a smile.
Fear isn't when you cower and shrink each day,
it's when your existence is nothing but vile.

Hate isn't when you loathe someone,
it's when your presence is an intrusion.
You aren't you when you practice caution,
it's when you unfurl your dreams and live with compassion.

3. CASTAWAY

Cloaked in a flight of fantasy,
it's only you, I can hear and see.
Astray in a tranquil hideaway,
not me, but my tears will find their way.

Marooned by my clueless desire,
it's only you who calls me a liar.
Brazen steps, alone and castaway;
not me, but my words will find their way.

Beguiled into a forgotten frame,
it's only you who can set me aflame.
Frozen warmth shadows and chills my day;
not me, but my smile will finds its way.

Collided space of past, present and future;
it's only you who can end this rumour.
Prey to blame, with no hideaway;
not me, but my heart will softly tread away.

4. DOWN TO MY KNEES.

I hear,
you're voice tickle my ear,
like a fleeting kiss.
A faint whisper,
let go! Its over.

I hear,
my heart plead,
don't place your want over need.
I am breaking,
stop loving him over me, quit waiting.

I hear,
my mind cajole,
you're strong, don't let him belittle your soul.
I am hurting,
stop loving him over me, quit waiting.

I hear,
hear you all.
broken from the fall,
I undressed my mind, left it bare.
I showed you my weakness,
thinking you would care.
But you left me a mess,
coming and leaving as you please,
bringing me down to my knees.

5. CONFINES OF YOUR MEMORY

I dreamt of you not so long ago,
restless and weary from staying apart.
Confines of your memory continue to grow,
as silence clamours and hammers my heart.

That miserable dawn of rain and cold,
reminiscent of bloody lies and kindred fights.
weak will, crushed beneath the train of thoughts;
alas, a cheerful soul, six feet under as secrets unfold.

They say, only time will heal;
the discreet wounds and emotions I conceal.
But their empty words console me no more,
for your absence resides in my existences core.

6. ENTREAT MY NEST OF LIES

I entreat my nest of lies,
and paper cut mangled family ties.1
Must I leave or must I stay?
How much do my memories, really weigh?

Abandoned dreams for others sake,
purpose divine washed off with tears and soap
Sleepwalking over an invisible ray of hope,
how much more will my breath take?

Vicious circle of gold, embedded around my finger,
innocent touch of love refuses to linger.
Promise of till death do us apart, I confess are lost.
How despicable, what does my happiness cost?

Suddenly, shadows weigh more than my worth,
and my rights are mute to your deaf heart.
Whom do I implore to end this feud?
How much more can my presence intrude?

I can trade my soul if you lend me the secret,
To braid the loop and mend the time we met.
Sunken ship with treasures of love and trust,
how do I wander away from your betrayals of lust?

7. DO YOU KNOW?

My little baby brother, younger by ten,
left too soon, to be in heaven.
Without you, my days are cold and quiet.
Wish I had held you for longer, when we last met.
Now, you're lying down unwilling to feel or cry,
yet I leave you roses, and continue to try.
I wear your memories on my sleeve, coloured with your brightest smile.
Adventurous to my little one, as he remembers you awhile.

I picture you with your heart warming smile,
full of mischief, love and care.
I wish I could hold you a while,
and unburden the pain you alone endure and bear.

Unknown to all, on your birthday each year;
I'll blow you a kiss.
Unsaid to all, on my birthday each year;
Do you know whom I miss?

8. IS LOVE KIND?

Some wounds seen, some collide the mind.
Is love patient, is love kind?
Some words harsh, some actions loud;
does love not envy, is it not proud?

Why do I dream of sunshine while in pouring rain,
if love does not delight in evil, but rejoices with the truth.
Why do I choose silence while in pain,
does love not protect, does it not trust?

Lost is my soul, that no longer feels.
Who says, love always hopes, always perseveres?
Hurt is my heart, that no longer loves.
Who says, love never fails?

9. PAIN THAT BEARS NO NAME

My heart that beat just for you,
has now split in two.
As paper boat dwindles in pouring rain,
I live with a pain that bears no name.

Father, mother, and a parent,
your birth gave us a new name.
Infinite possibilities, yet an unaltered moment.
Now we live with a pain that bears no name.

Loss of a baby, teen or a grown up;
an ache that overflows the bearers cup.
Widow and orphan, might suffer the same;
but, I live with a pain that bears no name.

10. WILL YOU?

Hello, will you hug me?
asked a dream from under a pillow.
I could once soar in the open sky,
now do you know, where dreams die?

Stay, will you kiss me?
asked love, from the arms of her beloved.
Shall I shower you with hearts riches,
or leave with broken promises?

Goodbye, will you miss me?
asked a sigh and diverged in two.
One became breath,
While other chose death.

11. SPARE ME A BREATH

Rapunzel, Rapunzel, lend me your hair,
before I climb up the heavenly stair.

Angel, Angel, may I borrow your halo,
my dark crown has fallen low.

Doctor, Doctor, save me again,
before I succumb to this numbing pain.

Reaper, Reaper, spare me a breath,
lest grace returns before its time for my death.

12. RAVEN

A raven flew and followed me home,
it dint ask for a name nor my phone.
It sat alone,
like my heart's clone.
It saw the bruises on my soul.
It saw me lose my life's control.

Marking a silent presence,
for my absence,
a raven flew away from home,
it had no name, nor a gravestone.

13. BLACK ROSE BURNING DOWN

Under the hood of shame,
was it love or loneliness,
that made the rose lose her name.

Under the lustful touch,
was it fear or eagerness,
that made the rose lose her allure as such.

Under the prying eyes,
was it hunger for skin or lies,
that made the rose lose her pride.

Under the crumpled sheets,
was it her nakedness covering him,
that made her neither proper nor prim.

A meddler, amongst a pair of doves.
A keep, an open talk of town.
Black rose burning down,
in the arms of one she loves.

SUN KISSED

14. NIL TO SPARE

In future who shall know my thought,
got lots to wear but nil to spare.
I'm broke today, tomorrow not,
I'll spend, I'll spend without a care.

Discounts and sales, now are my game,
I'm shopping heaps, why don't I know?
New bags, new shoes, they call my name,
too much to hold, can't keep nor throw.

I'm home at last to face my doom,
my money's gone, no food to warm.
I bought and bought but have no room,
I skip a meal and blame the norm.

From clothes, to shoes, to bags, I love,
got heart that beats, no soul to care.
No hope, for me to rise above,
I'll spend, I'll spend without a care.

15. COME FALL IN LOVE WITH ME

Every breath I take,
asleep or wide awake,
cant help but wish for you,
to come fall in love with me.

In dreams we meet,
with open eyes we depart.
Come ease my broken heart,
make me complete.

Under the twinkling stars,
and spellbinding moonlight,
come let me hold you tonight,
as, all of mine is yours.

Come let me adore you,
so that you can see,
cant help but wait for you,
to come fall in love with me.

16. FOOLS FAKE WORLD

Mirror, mirror on the wall;
can't you hear me shout and call?
Bountiful beggars and the homeless rich.
Reversal of fortune, an inevitable switch.
Rogue wandering shadows, lie to all.
Can they really break one's fall?

Glued to a Pandora's box,
life fabricated with lies and hoax.
Lured into a spiral downfall of ignorance,
surplus garb of the rich and famous.
Vain wagers in a fool's fake world.
Likes, shares, are binding spells carelessly hurled.

Online nemesis, befalls me, her and him,
Squandering time, aimless to the brim.
A lonely hearts delusional plan,
akin to strangers, dead to clan.
Mirror, mirror on the wall;
the one I see, isn't me at all!

17. TEA CUP THAT STOOD STILL

Over the moon and down the hill,
I spotted a tea cup that stood still.
Beaten on luck, a lazy clan of three,
unwilling to move, whatever it might be.

Failing eyes goaded the elder to foresee.
My back hurts, how can you ask me?
Fighting deadlines, father altered to a demon.
Where is my cup of tea, to rid this exertion?

Mind-numbing studies, left son teary eyed;
it possibly cant be me, I need to hide!
Humorous to some, torturous to few.
Over the moon and down the hill,
I spotted a tea cup that no one could fill.

18. BEWARE

Love me or hate me,
You are two-faced, so I don't care.
Praise me or shame me,
Your words are wasted, so beware!

A fathers pride, you're a girl, a mirror of glam.
But, the sun sees through your hide, and its all a sham.
A husbands heart, you're a woman, his inner muse.
But, the moon pleads through silence, baring recluse.

You're people's hope, a traitor, who sold her mother tongue.
Yet, when you speak, across 7 seas your tradition resounds.
A families faith, you're a tease, who couldn't hold down her hem.
Yet, when you dress, an echo of your culture and every heart pounds.

Restraints of your thoughts, retain you as a prisoner.
Complaints of your soul, deem you as a stranger.
Though, I am you and you are me.
You're immured in darkness but I am free.

19. MY MOTHER, WHOM I HATE THE MOST

My mother! Whom I hate the most,
she stalked my life, like a parasite and its host.
over broken dreams, I wept and wept,
until I gave up and silently slept.
My mind, my life; wasn't mine any more,
my mind was stuck shipwrecked on a shore.
Glum and mute, wounds caused by a double edged knife,
her choices I endured, to cast my life.

As I peer through an old doors crack,
time has broken her mind and back.
Over misunderstood dreams, I wept and wept;
until I realised and silently slept.
With a mired memory in a bottomless pit,
my name, my face is all that she knows, lost is her wit.
My mother! Whom I love the most.
Her choices I treasure, without her I am lost.

20. UNAWARE

My heart loves,
but never asks why.
My eyes dream,
but never see the sky.
My arms embrace,
but never feel the warmth.
My mind awaits,
but never knows what it wants.

Softly, the wind whispers,
lean in closer, it offers,
is it the secret it reveals,
or the mystery it conceals?
Like a drop of morning dew,
a sight to fortunate few,
I yearn to find the key,
unaware, its hidden within me.

21. UNSEEN VIEW OF US

Every time you smile,
my heart hums and a love story begins.
Every time you walk by,
my heart flutters like the butterfly's wings

What is this feeling?
So vast, like the sleepy blue ocean.
What is the reason?
So clear, like the spirit of clouds in motion.

Every time you smile,
my heart gleams its brightest glow.
Every time you walk by,
my heart beats its loudest crescendo.

Is this an unseen view of us?
Masked, like the magic of mountains.
Is this unrequited love?
Veiled, like all the untold emotions.

22. ONLY FOOLS RUSH IN

Only fools rush in,
wise never stay.
when broken hearted,
where do tears hide,
where does a smile reside?
Under the wings of an angel,
can my heart unfurl?
If I turn back time,
Can my heart unfurl,
under the wings of an angel?
Where does a smile reside,
where do tears hide?
When not in love,
wise never stay,
only fools, rush in.

23. KISS ON THE RUN

I asked my love,
why do we kiss, while on the run,
but never under the sun?
why do we hesitate,
isn't it love, or is this hate?

What do you say, my love
can we keep what we have,
or let go of the memories we wove?
Why do we hold,
so many secrets untold?

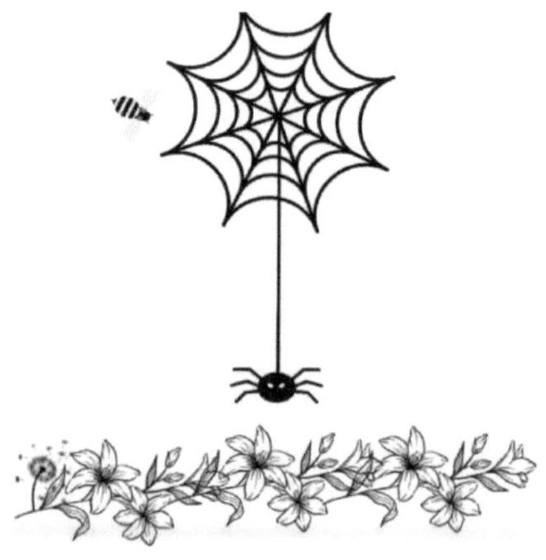

Even if you wait a while
nothing will change,
said my love, with a smile.
you know I am a cheat, isn't it strange,
Is that cause you yourself, are one?

24. WHO AM I?

Who am I?
without my cocoon.

Who am I?
without, what you assume.

Who am I?
without my wings

Who am I?
without borrowed things

I am a daughter,
I am a wife,
I am a mother,
I am life.

25. FRIEND OR FOE

Are you a friend or my foe,
asked a philanderer to his soul.
Does my touch awaken you,
or does it leave you feeling blue?
With held breath, soul whispered back,
I long for love, but you for lust,
Who's to blame me for mistrust,
when, what I need is all that you lack.

26. MELLOW EMBRACE

A shadow walks before me,
whose I know not.
Slumped shoulders and furrowed brows,
light by her feet, darkness within.
Boundless thoughts, who knows;
where she has been.

A shadow walks before me,
whose I know not.
empty hands and a tranquil heart,
mellow embrace of a fragrant rose,
timeless truth, who knows;
in accord, yet always apart.

A shadow walks before me,
whose I know not.
barefoot and forgotten as she goes,
averse to speak, reluctant to lead.
An endless path, who knows,
is it me, or you in my stead?

WHISPERING WISHES

27. I WISH I WAS JUST MY OWN

Forged in fire a heart so tender.
Yet, an accustomed liar whom no one can decipher.
Forgotten wings and a borrowed dream,
lost tears and a silent scream.

Many sunsets over my wristwatch,
and a closed door to face.
Like a child's game of hopscotch,
a futile attempt to find my place.

Mistaken as a daughter, wife and a mother,
born with a name but buried with another.
A dream, to belong to none.
I wish, I was just my own.

28. EVERYWHERE AND IN EVERYTHING

I am the beacon of hope, in a saddened heart.
I am the gleam of faith, that keeps you from falling apa
I am the courage that helps you stand against your foe.
I am the warm spring after rain and snow.

I am the fleeting joy in a birds first flight.
I am the calm after a storm on a peaceful night.
I am the answer to your every prayer.
I am the belief that teaches you to love and care.

I am the essence of your life's core.
I am the maker of every mysterious morning.
I am the one who loves you forever more.
For, I am everywhere and in everything.

29. REMEMBER ME

Remember me like the rain on a sunny day.
Remember me like a friend who has found her way.
Remember me like a nostalgic bittersweet dream.
Remember me like a child's gaze and its wondrous gleam.

Remember me like the magic of forever love.
Remember me like the twinkle of stars above.
Remember me like the fragrance of parched soil greeting the first rain.
Remember me like a happy song, until we meet again.

Remember me long after I am gone.
Remember me, for in you I live on.

30. EVERY HEARTBEAT

For every clock, there are infinite hours.
For every galaxy, there are a billion stars.
For every rainbow, a million raindrops fall.
For every word, a thousand thoughts recall.

For every king, there are a hundred slaves born.
For every rose, there is more than one thorn.
For every prayer, there are ten crossed fingers.
For every love story, there are 2 keepers.

For every dream there is one voice,
For every heart there is one choice,
Hearts that resided in two,
now beat as one in sync anew.

31. SOMEWHERE OVER THE RAINBOW

Summers gone and winter's far,
you look mystical to the gazing star.
Fiery leaves alight the autumn weather,
enticing colours than ashen white.
Fragrant winds call and whisper each night,
meet me in my dream and I'll love you forever.

A wish, I wish for you;
dew drops of joy over a dandelion or two.
With closed eyes, under the wings of an angel,
drape me in warmth from the numbing spell.
As a rose blushes, in embrace of pearly winter,
hold me in my dream and I'll love you forever.

Tender kisses of the morning sun,
melt down onto the bright yellow bloom.
When in love, it can never be undone,
an undying promise of the bride and groom.
As showers of paradise cassia in golden summer,
find me in my dream and I'll love you forever.

Somewhere over the rainbow, is a silent prayer.
as scorched land looks up to the misty eyed sky,
she yearns for him and he longs for her,
soon ends the long hiatus with a collective sigh.
Mesmerised by the fragrant haze of petrichor,
stay in m dream and ill love you forever.

32. PINCH OF SALT

Wish me luck,
don't hold me back.
Armed with a ladle,
and a pinch of salt,
I am off for a battle.
to temper hunger to a halt.

Boil, simmer, poach and steam;
fierce heat and whistling scream.
Root vegetables, camouflaged in earthen clay,
My trusted comrades, all fall prey.
Slice, dice, chop and mince;
ambushed fruits await their fate, post a rinse.

Sauté, sear, brown and char;
fragrant dishes on the kitchen bar.
Tuck and roll the resting dough,
Bring out the rolling pin for a final blow.
Fridge laden with jams, jellies, sauces and herbs;
glare and threaten the one, who disturbs.

With a new dawn,
I'm no more than a pawn.
Yet, armed with a ladle,
and a pinch of salt,
I am off for a battle,
to temper hunger to a halt.

33. PLASTIC ROSES

It crossed my mind,
a million times,
a bird never seeks,
delight or sorrow.
It just unfurls its wings,
unaware of tomorrow.

It crossed my mind,
a million times,
a rose never chooses,
life over death.
It simply mesmerises,
from the arms of a lover or a wreath.

It crossed my mind,
a million times,
a man never lives,
void of love and dreams.
Yet, admires the beauty of a caged bird,
surrounded by plastic roses of this world.

34. ONE

One
word.
One thought,
it's all that I need,
to make a new start.
I might fail or I might fall.
But, I will never give up, nor give in.
I might slouch, I might crawl,
to learn, to love my skin.
Now all that I need
is, one you
and one,
Me.

35. POCKET FULL OF STONES

At 20 past 12, while hopping in the air,
you show up with a surprise to share.
I hear Mrs. Simon say,
Oh! Its been such a lovely day.
But, aren't you a naughty little brat,
while others ferry their bag of books,
you jump around with, pocket full of stones,
saying, these here are whole of my heart.

I fall deeper for your charms,
as baby scent wafts off of your head.
Sleepy eyes find their way,
to nestle in the nook of my arms.
So close, that
I can hear my own heart.
Who says you're a naughty little brat,
Cause you here, are whole of my heart.

36. CARRY ME FAR AWAY

Carry me far away amongst the clouds,
away from the stares of stifling crowds,
until tears are but a distant dream.
Towards the horizon,
until dusk becomes dawn.

Carry me far away amongst the flowers,
away to a place which is only ours,
until our hearts mirror the celestial stars.
Towards fragrant flowers that kiss the warm twilight,
until we become one, and melt into the night.

37. MOVING DUNE

Walk through the mist of misunderstanding,
stop raking evanescent embers of the past,
as one who hurts shall heal at last.
Step away from loneliness and longing,
and silently bask under the glowing moon.
Though no obstacle can be held in an iron cast,
Look unto the wind, that shapes the moving dune.

38. I SURRENDER

I blow lightly to soothe your wound, pray softly without a sound,
Secrets, worries, fears, I kiss and tuck them all,
away in bags under my weary eyes.
I shoulder your beaten mind, caress your fatigue and embrace your aching heart.
Spine on my back, woven deep within my flesh,
cajoles my heaving bosom, to ease your pain.
My body, my soul, my mind, I thought was my own.
Your words, your hands, your love, say I was wrong.
In the cradle of our hearts line, cushioned by our joined palms,
I surrender! I surrender my all.

39. TWO TO LOVE

If you'd follow an ant, you'd find its sugar.
If you'd follow a boy, you'd find his treasure.
Once there lived such a boy and his tree.
This is their love, this is their story.
Not soon after, a beauty walked into their peace filled lives.
She was greed, she brought in hunger, fire and knives
Bit by bit the tree fell apart,
Until nothing was left, no body, no soul and no heart.
Blinded by greed, he chose wrong over right.
It wasn't the tree, but the boy who died that night.
The tree that was taken, was lost forever
The boy that was left was now a monster.
Furniture cant turn back nor can money make a tree.
Yet, the seeds from the tree, thought different, and wandered free.
They sang together, as their branches interwove,
It takes two to love.
One to live,
and other to forgive.

Thank you

9 798885 215930

Printed by Libri Plureos GmbH in Hamburg, Germany